Sound
Mind

A Collection of Poetry

Sound Mind
T.J. Singh

Contact Info: TJSingh.Poetry@gmail.com
- Thank you for your time and support. Feel free to use
the above email for contact. Appreciate any form of
feedback or discussion.

Table of Contents
Sound Mind

Miscellaneous Poems

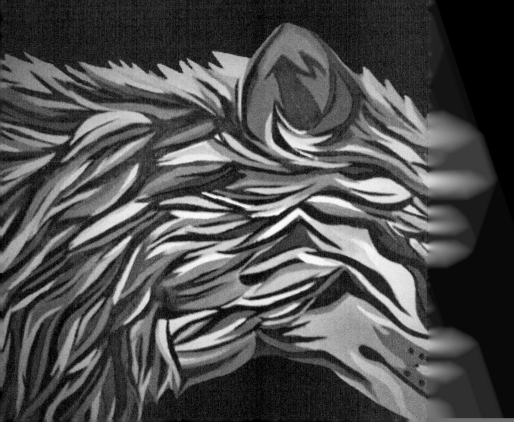

The Birth of Colour

A litter is born
on a quiet and warm winter.
Luna has conceived
without a whimper.
In peace and solitude,
with two newfound souls.
Blind and deaf
but fated to roam.
The newborns will grow
at a hastened pace.
To be like their elders and quickly join the race.

In a fortunate den,
which will be long forgotten.
The pups are spoiled with milk
as their eyes begin to blossom.
Inevitable predators,
yet born with innocence.
Soothed by their mother's breathe,
and safe from dissonance.
One daughter, one son.
Two delicate creatures.
Both grand in ancestry and only small in features.

All to carry burdens,
heavier for the one unalike.
For Aura's born with all colours
and life will be warlike.
Mothers do their best
and Luna is no different.
She'll raise them tender,
wise and militant.
Out of the den
and into the valley.
All is soundless on the ridge as they tip toe to their family.

The Valley

As the pups tip toe,
they notice the rituals of spring.
How the ice gives way
and rivers begin to sing.
Nature's melody rings out,
subtle and everlasting.
Birds all in harmony
and never distracting.
No puzzles to piece,
no forced bindings.
One is all, in these surroundings.

A pin drop in the snow
could be heard in the valley.
The birds lost their voices
and whispered sadly.
The signs began to stand out,
Luna began to run with force.
Her pups struggling to keep up
as she was taken by the source.
The pack was huddled.
Luna was lashed by fear.
She at once lost her senses and began to tear.

Her other half,
bleeding and rotting.
Ruthless was the valley,
that Luna had forgotten.
Nova's spirit was still strong
but his body nearly deceased.
He was ravaged and maimed
for sticking up to the Beasts.
He rallied a smile
and whispered not to cry.
Ecstatic at the safety of his family, as Luna kissed him a reply.

Luna: "O Nova,
    please meet our babes.
    They will grow with our love
    and the lessons from our tales.
    Dharma looks most like you
    and she has your cunning.
    A howl already fierce
    and a mind of hunting.
    Aura looks like all
    but with colours that don't fit in.
    A child of dreams that sings from within."

Nova: "Luna my all,
    I must address you first.
    It's not my new mutilations
    but the belief of losing you that hurts.
    I was trapped and lost,
    when you were gone.
    Departed was peace,
    all I had was my brawn.
    You now triumph over me,
    just like Mother Nature.
    Forever strong and your affection is my savior."

Nova: "I will get up for you,
    as you would for me.
    I will get up for my pups,
    even if I must live on my knees.
    My children,
    you will be my greatest fear.
    Evil feasts on the young,
    that is why the Beasts will always be near."
    (My future,
    why do you haunt me?
    The past is dead now, let the present hear this plea.)

Nova stood up,
with a smile and a limp.
No matter the tide,
he will captain this ship.
The other wolves ascended with joy
and began to howl.
A new hierarchy led by intellect,
as strength only soured.
Nova: (We will all be one.
A perfect circle moving forward.
We will not give in, as we cannot be cornered.)

Alpha Nova

Lost battles
and lake like scars.
Victories painted on
brittle clay jars.
How quick legends fade
but heroes stay the same.
Of the same cloth,
useless are their names.
So many have come,
and left the door open.
Our humanity, the quilt that is continually woven.

Luna told costly tales
about their poor father,
hardly survived
and initiated slaughters.
Born of his strength,
born of his weakness.
Nova plays his part
but longs for peace ceaseless.
Aura, Dharma,
Luna and Nova,
A new family, a box of Pandora.

Nova's path wasn't easy,
deserted in this winter sea.
He was left to rot,
like a leaf with no tree.
His family deemed him weak
and he began to wander.
Finally finding Luna,
he began to dream stronger.
Adopted and accepted,
Nova made the decision.
Leading this pack will be his only religion.

The Samsaras,
drifting through existence.
Mundanely being
and showing little resistance.
Thoroughly evolving
as they began to ask questions.
Why not change?
Why keep this grey reflection?
That's when they began
dancing and howling music.
Singing songs of a savior, to snap out of this illusion.

The Molocks

These beasts,
that guard the Devil and his bed.
These beasts,
that priest pretend to contain in their heads.
These beasts,
that only ever want to be fed.
These beasts,
that are obese off red wine and no bread.
These beasts,
that are drowned in a sea of red.
These beasts, that leave us blind and misled.

Luna dreaded
teaching of the beasts.
Them that will eat
most her children's feasts.
Born of violent red
and eyes of anger.
Society's sickness,
the world's new cancer.
Boisterous and sadistic.
The Molocks.
Evil so real yet unrealistic.

The same leader,
with no plans to change.
They thrive
when all stays the same.
The burning forest
and the starving child.
All symptoms
of their handcrafted wild.
Always in clusters,
rotten diseases.
When the core is weak, a virus does what it pleases.

The Molocks took over Yellowknife
with lies of prophecy.
Invisible action,
but words so heavy.
The wolves were out hunting,
they churned their lies.
Abusing the innocent,
destroying their minds.
Lies don't plant
and grow like trees.
They hover like clouds and spread like flees.

The Molocks built an empire
with Abraxus on top.
A swine with a serpent tongue,
that stood like a rock.
The other creatures,
they were practically nameless.
No true meaning,
life without sensation.
These pigs have ruled for years,
a crooked system that is strong.
They could uphold terror without lifting an arm.

Silent Treaties

Peace among
the starving poor.
Cities are woven by hands
that are sore.
The beaten down know,
vanity fades like all fabrics.
So they create with their hands,
survival's lone habit.
Silent treaties,
no signatures or crowns.
Just hard work building new towns.

Nova understood,
change always crawls slowly.
Understood this change will need
to breathe a different story.
To work with the other animals,
who are all on the same page.
Those who are hungry
and wish to devour this cage.
Nova: (I will start with the birds,
they've always been the closest.
They've seen the suffering and are trapped to just notice.)

Nova: "You ease us into our days,
and ornament our trees.
So we try to acknowledge you
in all our melodies.
Thank you for your songs
and distant friendships.
I wish to ask for your help
in retrieving all our senses.
These beasts take all our bread
but together we can stand strong.
We may all suffer at first but that is usually the start of a good song."

Birds in "Our friends,
unisom: you have always caught our eye.
　　　　The way you work hard
　　　　just to barely get by.
　　　　Our friends,
　　　　we'll always enjoy singing to you.
　　　　How you manage to paint with colours
　　　　even when you are blue.
　　　　We will be honoured to help,
　　　　we will spread your prayer.
　　　　We're all different but we reside in the same air."

Nova: "We will build a village
　　　　and fight together.
　　　　We will play the beast's games
　　　　and we'll play them clever.
　　　　Pain's voice…
　　　　that silent whimper.
　　　　We won't lose our voice,
　　　　even if we must whisper.
　　　　Now let's win this war
　　　　that we did not start.
　　　　Let's fight back by not tearing each other apart."

Village Called Kingdom

It is July
but it's feeling like December.
Another day gone by
with nothing to remember.
I was told to build this village
with no bricks or cement.
I guess I'll use the dirt
that's clogged in my head.
One day at a time,
it will all be done.
I'll end where I started, my father's son.

Nova decided
he would build a new village.
They were all divided
even if the lines were hidden.
All he had to do
was promise the beasts,
he would build them a temple
for their holy feet.
Nova: (We will keep cover
in this disguise.
Playing to their egos, we will salvage our lives.)

The animals danced
while they diligently built.
Their work was hard
but their attitude held the hilt.
The village was made in days
but would last centuries.
Hidden and everlasting
like childhood memories.
Nova: (We've made a compromise.
Let's see how long this lasts.
May we live in peace even if we contrast.)

Voice

It whispers, it cracks,
it screams, it's you.
It is the savior
worshipped by very few.
Your grasping mind's
fingerprint.
It matches
your eye's glint.
To find it,
is gold.
Lose it, your truth won't be told.

Luna: "Your voice is yours
but it belongs to the people.
It can cure or destroy
just like the needle.
Singing is a tradition,
but to some it is a calling
My little pup.
The world will hear your howling.
Let us not give up
but sacrifice everything.
When we sing we can catch God's eye peaking in."

Luna: "Now close your eyes
and breathe into your stomach.
Visualize nature's smoke,
in you humming.
Let those vibrations
ripple the waters.
Let the smoke
become your vowels.
Now I know
it's not always the case,
but smile and let the silence in you vibrate."

Aura: "My howls not like yours
        or fathers.
        How can I be the one
        to ripple these icy waters?
        I feel like a sideshow,
        with all these colours.
        I wish to fit in
        like the Sun in the summer.
        Maybe as I grow,
        I'll turn to grey.
        How bad could it be to just turn away?"

Luna: "Like the Sun?
        Have you looked in the sky?
        There are colours you cannot count
        with your eyes.
        You are free
        and you will always be.
        A lamb fierce as a lion,
        that is what you'll achieve.
        Peace with yourself
        and all your neighbours around you.
        The fog will always clear at your rendezvous."

Youthful Praise

Loved
and then forgotten.
Young
and then rotten.
Sharp
and then bloodied.
Tortured
and then studied.
Forced speech
and no words sung.
Story of some, except those that learn to die young.

It began with folk tales,
turned into folk songs.
Lyrics that all could sing,
you couldn't do it wrong.
A voice not strong
but daring.
Lyrics to leave all
but evil soaring.
Bisons, Grizzlies,
Coyotes and Blue Birds.
All tied together with a golden string of words.

Aura was praised,
loved as a youth.
No forced occupation,
just living the truth.
The entire town would smile
at the child's sheen.
How real the laughter,
happiness didn't need to be achieved.
One with the wheel,
one with the road.
Received charitably, even after the beasts were owed.

The swine wanted more,
not just a piece of the bread.
They craved for their souls
and then their flesh.
The child would sing for all beings
and entertained all the folk.
The whole town in awe,
even the beasts would choke.
The plot then began to form.
Molocks: "We can't give the wolves more power.
This child has inspired, and left our fear devoured."

The Plot

The loud fiends
and their quiet deeds,
murder us whole
with their needs.
Leeches are
forever hungry
and latch on
to our knees.
We are outnumbered
in the cold darkness.
Look at them huddled around your mother's carcass.

Jinn: "They've learned;
        the right and left isn't born
        but a riff in the center
        which we adorned.
        The mast ocean of concrete,
        we created with our lies.
        We mustn't let them multiply,
        we must uphold this divide.
        It started with the strength of Nova
        and the love of a Mother.
        Passed on to their youngest, who wanders like no other."

Apopsis: "We mustn't worry,
          what we say always goes.
          We crack the whip
          and it is their freedom that we hold.
          We must stick to our roots,
          it is what got us here.
          We will cause chaos
          and slyly disappear.
          What better way
          then muzzling the young?
          The right hand feeds and the left removes their tongues."

Abraxus: "Suffering isn't complex,
all it takes is a simple plan.
We'll up the food tax,
the young will hunt due to our hand.
Too busy working,
they will lose their voice.
Enough to keep their skin
and believe they have a choice.
We've done it before
and we will do it again.
We will mask our true nature and pose as wise men."

Abraxus: "Here's a toast to us,
now let us dance in this fire.
We'll blacken and char
all that they admire.
All the art they created,
we will turn it into dust.
Slow slaughter,
their minds will be crushed.
The child will lose himself,
when he begins to hunt.
He will work for us and all his colours will rust."

Dust in the Eyes

A gathering of the good,
the wicked are salivating.
Distractions of the tongue.
Flattery becomes suffocating.
Feet of the good dangling,
the rotten comfy in their seats.
Evil has no colour,
only black and white beliefs.
Truth in all sides,
we're conveying our own stories.
Except the few, that don't answer to inquiries.

Abraxus: "My friends,
I've asked that you all be here.
We must discuss our future.
Please lend us your ears.
You've all grown in numbers
and we've nurtured your growth.
We've protected you these years,
we've all taken the oath.
Now this is no deception,
but we fear there are bigger beasts.
For us sages to stay strong, our feasts must increase."

Every animal in silence,
there was nothing they could do.
Some believed in bigger beasts,
others already knew.
The meek blinded by fear.
They'll work to save their treasures.
Their backs have been belted
and they'll be labored by this leather.
The innocent and frightened
nervously began to cheer.
Not knowing from this point, they will never see clear.

Hunting

You should've seen,
what I saw on my way.
The hungry eating the hungry
in broad day.
Smacked slaves
working for scarce wages.
All colours
and all ages.
You should've seen,
what I saw on my way.
One being trampled on for trying to get away.

Nova started with his first lesson;
How to control your breath.
Nova: "Breathe the fire into your stomach
and exhale with breadth.
Instruct your mind to inhale,
use your thoughts as whips.
Exhale slowly
and feel time pass your lips.
It'll come with practice,
as all things do.
This lesson is essential; it is life's glue."

Dharma: "Father,
I'm not trying.
This isn't it,
this isn't fighting."
Nova: "Hunting isn't violence,
it's nature's work of art.
To do what is necessary
and thoughtfully play your part.
We evolved through morals,
we do not hunt to hurt.
We evolved through family, we hunt solely to support"

Aura: "Father I've done this before,
       It's how Mom taught me to sing.
       Makes it more excruciating,
       I don't wish to do anything."
Nova: "Hurts me as much as it hurts you,
       I too dream of your dreams.
       Creation twist and shakes,
       progress is never what it seems.
       You will always have our support,
       even when your voice is gone.
       Take in all experiences, turn every moment into song."

Nova: "The second lesson;
       One pointedness.
       The key is concentration
       and I want you to remember this.
       Focus on your own goal
       and never get caught in another.
       We have power over ourselves,
       never over others.
       Treat your past failures as water,
       required for you to grow.
       Your mind is as a flower, and that is all you'll ever need to know."

Nova: "The third lesson;
       Is knowing when to act.
       Time is always crucial,
       but you do not have to be exact.
       Simply be present
       and listen to all your senses.
       Your mind will trample all,
       it can't be fenced in.
       The mouth is fed of those,
       who do not doubt.
       Confidence is born to all; you have to learn to let it out."

Dharma: "I get it now
and I'll begin to practice.
To calm the mind
and know when to be active."

Aura: "I get it too
and I'll follow suit.
I'll keep life in balance
and be absolute."

Nova: "Life is precious for all,
so we only hunt for a living.
Remember, there is only one end and one beginning."

Rusting

How quickly we forget,
the colours that are born.
The self is forgotten,
when a uniform is worn.
The colours rust,
with every menial task.
Dreams fade away
and rot behind a mask.
Truth hidden in our closets,
we live in our horrors.
The artist in you dies and turns into a forger.

Love slowly soured
into tasteless hate.
Aura became ill
in this uninspiring state.
A child once loved,
now considered a nuisance.
Too colourful to be stealthy
the other hunters became abusive.
Aura would turn
to Nova's knowledge,
breathe and don't allow hatred to take you hostage.

Aura remained patient
and began to persevere.
To see clearly that both time
and practice always adhere.
No God given talent
but here stands a new killer.
How outfits can change us,
when trapped in a mirror.
What has truly changed,
with this newfound success.
The beasts have gotten bigger and all are still depressed.

Dharma: "Here we both are
and I feel like I'm meant for this duty.
Please don't take this the wrong way
but seeing you here is cruelty.
Your voice sounds different,
and your colours are turning grey.
Your looking like all of us
and I can't stand to see you this way.
Please, I beg you to stop.
Let me be the one that hunts.
Sing of the beautiful meadow and don't join this battlefront."

Aura: "My colours are fading
and maybe that's how it should be.
I tried the other way,
an artist begging on his knees.
Society controls what I do,
I don't own a voice.
I'm here because they want me here,
I don't have a choice.
I'm greying now
and I'm no longer being abused.
I'll do as I'm told and keep myself subdued."

Luna's Fall

The fall is never the same,
some descend deeper.
A mother is vulnerable
as she feels her child's fever.
Sickness of the mind
burns like a wildfire.
The mind works overtime
as the body retires.
Despair the grave,
and your thoughts the shovel.
Life decays and we are the rubble.

Luna: (I wanted more for them,
and now I can only watch.
My young are now slaves
and are ruled by the clock.
I can't stand to be,
I don't have the will to remain.
I'll lock myself away
and breath in this pain.
From this day forward,
I won't dream a thing.
An icy winter with no sign of spring.)

Hear From Another

Bad things tend to happen,
they often even return.
How you hear about them
can amplify the burn.
We all lose things,
and only some know what.
Ties are slowly severed
and never so clear cut.
Loved ones wither away
and become like distant stars.
Burns to hear someone close is gone from someone so far.

The training was complete,
they'd mastered an ancient art.
Cold bloodied killers
with youthful hearts.
They will have to hear,
from a stranger in the pack.
That their mother has fallen,
with no signs of an attack.
Aura: "We will have to go back,
I can't believe the news.
How could she fall ill without a disease or bruise?"

Nova: "You used to sing about it,
don't you remember the blues?
Disturbing are those thoughts
like leeches that can chew.
She never wanted to see you hunt,
not at such a tender age.
The silent ones fall to sadness,
they have no will to rage.
How could I be so blind?
Not putting family before the chase.
The beasts have blinded my soul and left me defaced"

Aura: "I'm sure she's fine,
      We're doing what we're supposed to do.
      I'm sure it isn't bad,
      just rain passing through."
Dharma: "That's true,
      how bad could it be?
      We're all blessed with food,
      even after we give to the beasts."
Nova: "Denial deepens the grave
      and only resumes the digging.
      Your mother is going through hell without even sinning."

Nova: "We will turn back now
      with our chins up high.
      Your mother may be low
      but she is still worthy of the sky.
      I know what will cheer her up,
      one of those songs.
      The ones Aura used to sing
      and we would all hum along.
      That was the life she wanted,
      let us go back to her nest.
      May it quiet her nightmare and allow her to rest."

Suffering Tree

Silhouette trees
and shady smoke skies.
With winter's silence
and dark winds passing by.
No shade beneath this rootless tree,
the buddings have withered away.
Greens have turned brown
and muddy are the days.
Arms amputated
and only depression clings.
The landscape rots as maggots are crowned kings.

Their spirit's mirror image,
yet she has lost her reflection.
Her nature to nurture is still evident
in their heroic complexions.
They inched closer to her shelter
and their fears began to howl.
They could feel it from a far,
agonies silent growl.
Misery worked her magic,
and nailed all the windows shut.
You could tell despair was living in this lonely hut.

Dharma: "Mom,
        please wake up and let us see your face.
        Our eyes grew icy
        without your visions embrace."
    Aura: "I feel like a pup again,
        just being near your scent.
        All your lessons of love,
        distance taught me what they meant.
        We're hunters now
        but we will never lose your love.
        We're here now but we know that's not enough."

Luna turned to Dharma
and tears rolled down her cheek.
Luna: "You've grown so strong
as I knew you could be."
She turned to her bright star
but couldn't recognize a thing.
That's when she felt the illness,
that scorching sting.
Aura walked towards her
but she scampered away.
Luna: "I don't see my bright colours, just a mask of grey."

Luna: "Let me die in your old footsteps
and bright memories.
Let me die in peace
like a secluded tree.
Our circle has sharpened,
and I am cut by the edge.
You were the light encircling me,
now all I see is the ledge.
A voice that could soothe the clouds,
while parting the sea.
Prove you are my Aura by singing your songs for me."

Aura went to howl
and out crept a voice.
A complete stranger,
his mother wept at the noise.
Aura: (I don't remember my voice,
and have long forgotten my songs.
I can only recall the hunt
and all that I've done wrong.
This isn't me
and my mother knew it first.
I'll heal my family and slaughter this curse.)

Soaring

Listen to the Sun's crackle,
how it vibrates the wind.
The winter came screaming
but now it will rescind.
These rings you put on your fingers,
that only you can see.
Lock away your anxieties
and bury the key.
The start of your new life
is now.
Whatever you do will strengthen your vow.

Nova: "My child,
together we will right this wrong.
I will take care of your mother,
you remain headstrong.
Remember the old folk legend,
The Kudu of Change.
He paved the way for song,
his chords have not aged.
Traveled far 'n' wide,
and far within.
He shall be the one you seek; redemption will then begin."

Nova: "He began in this old valley,
and made it all that it is.
Wrote songs for all
and never pretended it was his.
There was no ownership,
we would all sit 'n' share.
Hunters still hunted
but they did it with care.
He was born of colour like you,
no soul considered him normal.
Yet his colours grew brighter and his music was crowned immortal."

Nova: "I want you to seek him
and be his apprentice.
It will not be easy,
treat it as your penance.
Legend has it,
that he awaits for one like him.
A cloud out in the sky
that has gone paper slim.
May you become whole
and discover what we all lost.
May you be the son that burns away the frost."

Scholarship

In this underground church
strength is earned.
You'll recognize to step over
and not on the worm.
A humble reader,
a frightening being.
You're ripening
all that you're reading.
Experience,
a wise drunk teacher.
A cure, for all of life's fevers.

Aura began to study
all of the tales of old.
How a speck of nothing
could grow into gold.
The tales spoke of an outcast
with hardly a voice.
He had conquered his words
and singing came with no choice.
A writer first
and a singer last.
Carried on old traditions but never mirrored the past.

Aura: (The books inform
that the kudu went up north.
A rock of forgiveness,
The Land of Rebirth.
Few make it past the sea,
most just stare from the shore.
No violence rampant,
yet there rages a war.
I'll journey my way
to that rampant sea.
The wisdom of the storm will guide and carry me.)

He continued to meditate
because Aura always knew.
The fault of all the dead dreamers
was the rush to get through.
Countless before
and many to attempt after.
Fame was their goal,
vanity was their rapture.
With one deep breath
and only one belief,
that attaining oneself will finally be achieved.

The Road

Off to the road
that was paved years ago.
The one that is travelled
silently alone.
Where the long grass
marks the path
and the yellow wood
never rots black.
Times changed
but the road, still the same.
One few will know and can never be named.

Aura travelled north,
with family on the mind.
A tight rope walk,
he could not look behind.
On this road he was met
with the fiercest of snow.
One that could bury
and happily mask a glow.
By keeping his eyes on his dreams
and his thoughts controlled.
He burned a fire within and slaughtered the cold.

Out came a voice,
not frightening but bold.
Voice: "You've made it this far
but can't continue alone."
Aura looked up
and he saw the wind blow.
There stood a glow
like a ghost of snow.
Trusting only on instincts,
Aura knew this soul was good.
Daedalus: "My name is Daedalus and you stand where I once stood."

Daedalus was made of snow
with melancholy eyes.
Eyes scarred by lost
and reddened of sacrifice.
Built like a mountain
yet hardly a form.
He was a builder by hand
with a mind of gold.
Legend has it,
he lost his sparkling son.
An artist whose mind had become undone.

Daedalus: "You remind me of my son
and I wish for redemption.
For I crafted him wings
and he turned the wrong direction.
He became wildly arrogant
and didn't heed my words.
Flew too close to the Sun
and his wings slowly burned.
I will craft your wings
but you must earn my trust.
I've been haunted by beasts playing with angel dust."

Aura: "I'm honoured to help
and I'm keen to fly.
I've dreamt of the moment
when howling at the sky.
I've seen you before
in one of my dreams.
I was told to disregard
but I would dwell on what they mean.
To me they always seemed
more real than the hunt.
Sorry I know, not all things are meant to be discussed."

Daedalus snapped his fingers
and it began to rain.
Like the stars became free
and threw down their chains.
Daedalus himself
transformed.
He became like water.
The ground then began to warm.

Daedalus: "The dark flood
will now surely rise.
I want you to embrace the waves and be one with the tide."

Aura: "I'm a wolf
and I'll lose all I've ever learned.
Who are the beasts
you spoke of before?"

Daedalus: "These beasts are similar
to the ones you know.
I had momentarily trapped them
and tried to contain them in snow.
Now it's your turn to fight
and I'll be your guide.
Now take these wings and keep your head up high."

Daedalus clapped his hands
and outgrew Aura's wings.
They bore naturally
and Aura didn't feel a thing.

Daedalus: "As you may have noticed,
you don't need the wisdom to fly.
Knowledge can sometimes be locked
and trapped inside.
Now these beasts also have wings
but not like yours.
For their wings torment but yours will cure."

Daedalus: "They will begin to appear
         and challenge you with force.
         You'll need to strike them
         and drown their depraved curse."
         The smiling heathen Astar appeared
         with a wicked red blush.
    Astar: "I've longed for you
         with a demonic lust."
         A battle ensued
         and Aura struck a ferocious blow.
         Astar's wings vanished and he drowned in the flood below.

         Where the beast fell
         turned to mucus and pus.
         The dark ocean evaporated the filth
         in a godlike rush.
    Aura: "What is this ocean?
         What of my home?"
Daedalus: "Your world is not affected,
         those lost souls still roam.
         This ocean I created
         and was hidden in my maze.
         I named the deep-sea Maya, an ocean that can blaze"

Forever

This war makes no sense
and it won't ever end.
Rotting flesh accumulates
where the river bends.
The worms and flies dance
on all nameless graves.
The lost souls are swept
by the violent blue waves.
Why not let go
and treat all places like home?
The thought is small but large like a toddler's gravestone.

Aura was still at war,
beast after beast.
No signs of tiring
but when will it cease?
Astar reappeared
with that same perverted smile.
Aura: "How could you be back?
You were the first of this pile."
Astar: "Why do you think I smile?
Can a thought ever die?
You've made me warmer, I live for this high!"

Daedalus showed no signs of worry
and even let out a chuckle.
Daedalus: "My Aura,
it's going to take more than muscle.
This maze isn't outside
but concealed in your mind.
These beasts represent you
and what you bury inside.
How do you stop feeding
these old and lonely beasts?
We will train your demons and you won't need a leash."

That's when Aura instinctively
took a bold stance.
Hovered with his eyes closed
and lowered his hands.
All the beasts reappeared
and spread around in a circle.
They began shouting, taunting,
bolstering that they were immortal.
Aura saw darkness,
an ocean of night.
He had entered a new world, and saw just a bit of light.

Aura: "Where am I?"
       Out thundered a bell like sound.
       A voice then followed,
Voice: "This is the artist's hunting ground."
Aura: "All I see is black
       and nothing of the senses."
Voice: "This is where you will create
       your brand-new dimension.
       You see,
       close your eyes
       and prepare for the final road."

       Aura thought of blue mountains
       and their icy glow.
       Aura thought of the rain
       and how endless a river flowed.
       There appeared a scene
       of ultramarine hues.
       There appeared the truth
       of what the mind could do.
Aura: (I will create here
       and control my destiny.
       I will create here and be as I wish to be.)

Aura opened his eyes
and all the beasts silently stared.
He let out a godly howl
and everything around him flared.
A ripple of light
with the sound of thunder,
cleared all beasts
and buried them under.
Daedalus: "There are many beasts,
train the ones that can't hurt you.
Let them sharpen your sword and see you through."

Daedalus: "I want you to know,
this only works on this road.
You will lose most of this power
when returning back home.
That isn't to scoff at,
you've made it this far.
Take these memories
and store them in life's jar.
These gluttons will not bother you,
but they will always roam.
They will find their way in some other poem."

Inner Voice

Language of Symbols
that save from sharp tongues.
Love beyond skin
that keeps our old habits young.
Sitting in our grey minds,
deep forests of rhymes.
Swimming in our thirst,
plentiful rivers of time.
The sky has more colours
than we can ever number.
The mind has more reflections then we can ever wonder.

Aura: (I'll stop throwing rocks at mountains,
      I once lived like such a fool.
      I'll keep this mind barren but beautiful
      and not be the Devil's tool.
      I'll continue marching forward
      and never look behind.
      I'll make progress
      by never obsessing over time.
      These thoughts are unique
      and hopefully not crazy.
      I mean I shouldn't worry, as long as I don't tell anybody.)

Crossed the Line

Where the lines cross,
that is where we meet.
To go in full circle
is a coward's defeat.
Nailed, battered, bruised;
all with the will to choose.
To comprehend one's story
and never refuse.
The crossroads,
where the voice is grown strong.
No saints just sinners turning sins to song.

Aura flew across the deep sea
with no doubts in his mind.
Daedalus disappeared
as he wished to stay behind.
That old road is his road,
it's his to show.
Aura respected his teachings
and all that he knows.
Aura set foot
on a new desolate shore.
Continued charging, he could feel there was so much more.

Aura didn't see it happen
but felt every moment.
The earth softened
and the trees became permanent.
The shade was openhearted,
 in this pure forest.
A place of relation,
all things bonded and nourished.
The birds sang differently,
almost in a choir.
Songs of freedom, not of deceiving desires.

Aura howled out
a happy tone.
Aura: (First time here,
but I feel so at home.)
Aura couldn't help it
and began to run with joy.
The wind caressed his ears
with a divine noise.
He found the largest tree
and rubbed his nose against it.
Aura: (This is what is needed, this is profit.)

The Blue Birds

This boat is balanced
that's why it will last.
Sailed the rockiest sea
and it never did crash.
I guess you had to
trust the wind.
I guess the sea
forgave your sins.
Now on a new shore
with the Sun shining on.
Time to paint over all the sketches, that you have drawn.

An acorn dropped
and grazed Aura's head.
A smiling voice rang out,
Voice: "How are you my friend?"
Aura responded with a smile,
Aura: "I'm well and how are you?"
Voice: "Well I am this tree
and to me there's nothing new.
Who are you
and what brings you to this point?"
Aura: "The Kudu of the North, I wish to hear his voice."

Out rang numerous laughs
and Aura opened his eyes.
There flew three blue birds,
all identical in size.
Blue "Did you really think trees could talk?
Birds: How high your hopes must be?
I mean if this tree could talk,
it probably wouldn't be so friendly.
I would hate to have someone
rub their snout on my skin.
Especially a wanderer, who knows where that's been."

The birds were childlike
but knew everything there was to know.
They introduced themselves as titles
and did proudly so.
The first, The Painter.
The second, The Comedian.
Then, The Actor.
Comedian: "Our names were only aliases."
Aura: "How can I trust liars,
who don't tell me their real names?"
Actor: "Think back to everyone you've known; don't they all do the same?"

Painter: "We'll show you around
and get to know each other.
There are no predators or prey here,
just sisters and brothers."
Aura: "That's beautiful
but what do you guys eat?"
Actor: "We all drink at the Lake of Vision,
we have no need for feasts."
Comedian: "We are all
successfully homeless.
We all live on the road, keeps us sheltered from loneliness."

Aura followed the blue birds
and couldn't believe what he observed.
The lake was surrounded by all creatures,
all free and unnerved.
They drank from the same lake,
yet no ripple effect.
They bathed in the lake,
yet no one would get wet.
No one paid any mind
and Aura began to sing.
Feeling only happiness, it's easy to become anything.

The First

You may not get fame,
or a new name.
But your sound will travel
just like the wind and rain.
They'll feel your blues
but only in secret.
The masses tend to hide,
we've all seen it.
Respect those before
and pave for those after.
Life is a joke and music is the laughter.

Actor: "Now to get the kudu's attention,
that is easy as it goes.
You create from your soul
and put on a show."
Aura: "I've only sung old melodies,
I'm sure the times have changed.
They would label my songs soft,
they would never get played."
Painter: "Don't sell yourself short,
we heard your songs when you were young.
They were bold and up here they were sung."

Comedian: "What's the first thing on your mind?
Come on just write it down.
Sad? Perverse? Angry?
Wear your thoughts as crowns."
Aura: "I'm angry my people are slaves,
I'm sad it'll never change.
I'm angry my father has fallen
and I'm sad my mother is now insane."
Painter: "You feel what everyone feels,
the world sadly relates.
The key is to be their voice and help carry their burden's weight."

Aura wrote the first song,
the "Nine to Five Blues".
The chords were simple,
and the lyrics reeked of booze.
Aura knew it was the one,
it could make a wander's callused feet tap.
You could pour out a drink
or maybe even get in a scrap.
With twelve bars,
the song had a powerful pedigree.
The song was fun and dirty, as life should be.

The Second

The first is rarely the last,
and it makes the second so real.
The first is heavenly and the second
is the Devil sealing the deal.
To write with the end in mind
and not falter.
To write your heart down
and never let it alter.
A second chance
is rarely ever given.
Except in art, where it is one's volition.

Now the blue birds left Aura
on a quiet and ancient hill.
Aura could feel a presence
but all was ever still.
Aura: (I've never felt this way,
almost as if I am being watched.
I don't sense any evil,
nor do I feel cold or hot.
I don't wish to jump to conclusions,
my mind is probably playing tricks.
I can almost feel souls but I don't think I'm allowed to admit.)

The Sun danced
and Aura began to write.
A folk song like old,
one with mostly bite.
It was written for the workers,
the ones that carry the heaviest load.
The ones who see the ends last,
and are not allowed to fold.
Aura: (This one is called "The Ground You Shook",
and I know it will resonant.
Both sides know its truths but only one will acknowledges it.

Burning

Eyes open, heart locked.
The burning may never cease.
The feelings come and go,
they eternally repeat.
Maybe if I write,
lust will turn to love?
Maybe if I sing,
they'll know where my pain comes from.
Two sides to all
but only one true self.
With all these trust issues, I can't even trust myself.

Aura on the same hill,
with closed wandering eyes.
Felt a new desire,
one that could only be denied.
Aura thought of love
and longed to meet another.
One who knew how to smile
but also how to suffer.
Fighting these thoughts,
only led to frustration.
The loneliness infected his new foundation.

Aura: (I'm in this heaven
with devilish thoughts.
How can I survive?
How will I come across?
All my feelings of love,
rot and turn to lust.
I've only ever imagined
and can't control the rush.
This next song will be it,
a call out to the one.
I'll title it "The Burning" and I'll point it like a gun.)

The Dam

Wake up every morning,
yet nothing really happens.
The ship is idle,
can we not blame the captain?
We've been at this for years
and now only our tools evolve.
The mind hasn't been stilled,
just beaten and scarred.
All it takes is one drop
and the rest will follow.
The ocean is forever moving from life's lonely vibrato.

Aura sat with his eyes closed
and let nothing happen.
Opened both eyes to write,
but all ideas dampened.

Comedian: "That happens to me all the time,
good thing life's a joke.
I usually go for a walk
and inhale all the smoke."

Painter: "I too reach that point
and usually turn to sketch.
Nothing great comes but it gives my mind a stretch."

Actor: "How much have you written?
Don't be surprised if it is enough.
You've already moved forward
by calling the oppressor's bluff."

Aura: "I've finished writing three songs
and I know the beasts will hear.
How I'm trying to get out, not in.
and dry my people's tears.
I've gone blank with ideas
and will practice what I have.
I'll polish every syllable and sharpen my attack."

Actor: "I can feel that you've grown,
　　　　this hill will do that to a soul.
　　　　This wasn't overnight,
　　　　you've been working to gain control.
　　　　I'll help set up the show,
　　　　you can open with your three songs.
　　　　We'll help you practice,
　　　　that's where it usually goes wrong.
　　　　Go get some rest by the river,
　　　　maybe make some friends.
　　　　They'll be the ones to carry you and help you meet your ends."

The River at Dark

Dreams mix with sand,
the sky and rivers swim in blue.
A large landscape
and in the center is you.
This night burns bold,
an undying heat.
The Sun will soon join in
and lift us to our feet.
We'll burn away our fears
and be free.
We'll sing our new song and let the clouds hear our plea.

Aura rested by the lake,
now coloured by the glowing Moon.
He could hear animals speaking,
all were in tune.
He spotted another wolf,
and began that burning feeling.
Aura's vision began to blur
and he could feel his soul beating.

Aura: (Those sly blue birds,
this all seems too perfect to be true.
Only one other wolf and she controls my view?)

Blue   "Ahhhh,
Birds: playing our Favorite Game?"
Painter: "She's a quiet soul,
we'd have to tell you her name."
Aura: "I wish to focus on my craft,
I can't be interested in her.
I just wish to have a drink,
now go be as you were."
Actor: "Your mouth spews one thing
but your eyes say another.
The game isn't about lust, it's about finding another."

Aura: "What is this game?
　　　　I can't tell if you're being serious."
Comedian: "All artists play it
　　　　and it's been destroyed by the idiots."
Painter: "The goal is to create
　　　　and let it guide you to love.
　　　　Going from town to town
　　　　and being the art you speak of.
　　　　The game is to try
　　　　and not break when you're stung.
　　　　It will help you write with a loaded gun."

Aura: "I'll go talk to her,
　　　　but please let it be on my own terms.
　　　　I don't wish for her to think of me,
　　　　as those perverted worms."
Painter: "Her name is Thothra,
　　　　she one day just appeared.
　　　　Writes, works as a healer
　　　　and in both her name is revered."
　　　　Aura glanced at her
　　　　and her dark purple complexion.
　　　　His anxiety spoke and scattered in all directions.

Ra

The other half is never
what it seems.
The other half is royalty
and glistens like a queen.
The torture to try
and be ourselves,
while society tries
to pull us into itself.
Stranded here,
where people eat people.
Let's feel each other's warmth, as it may be our only freedom.

Aura inched closer
and with a smile she observed.
A worker by his hands
and a struggler with spoken words.
Aura paused
and began to hum.
Thothra: "I love your colours,
where are you from?"
Aura: "I'm from the South,
a scenic place called Yellowknife.
Hard to describe, I would have to show it to your eyes."

Thothra: "I see,
thought you were all business and no play?"
Aura: "I play,
I just prefer on a page."
Thothra: "Arrogant and quiet wit,
a writer?"
Aura: "I prefer rambler,
the burden is a lot lighter.
I've been writing songs,
up on that aged hill.
Why don't you join me sometime, if you have time to kill."

Thothra: "I don't have time to kill,
        but I will be there.
        To hear your practice
        and prayer.
        I write myself
        but for my eyes only.
        Not all writers wish to write
        an identifiable story.
        Could you tell me about your people?
        Why leave your home?
        I don't come across wolves like me who roam all alone."

Aura: "My people…my people,
        they are all I've ever known.
        They work and work
        until blood leaves their bones.
        They've been tricked
        by charlatan beasts.
        Tactful verbiage
        coming from demonic teeth.
        My mother lost her head,
        seeing what I had become.
        I've traveled far to learn from the horned yet virtuous one."

Thothra: "I'll introduce you to my friends,
        that is all I can offer.
        They live simple lives
        and don't judge kings or paupers.
        They helped me when my life was on edge,
        all was so epic.
        They taught me that letting go
        can be the greatest weapon.
        We will work on helping your people,
        everyone together.
        For now let's be here, lets enjoy today's adventure."

Practice

The Sun's stretch
and the Moon's acclaim.
The same routine,
yet no day the same.
A creator creates,
preserves and destroys.
Killing old habits
and building with joy.
Countless days
where nothing happened,
led us to that day where everything happened.

Aura practiced for days
on that ageless hill,
a flute around his neck
and foot drums at his heels.
The blue birds cheered
at every mistake.
Comedian: "Get those out now,
and they'll never remain."
Aura could only smile,
Aura: (I've never thought of it that way.
Success as paradise and failure as the doorway.)

Then came Thothra,
pen and paper in hand.
She wrote from a distance
and struck him seldom with a glance.
Aura: (My anxiety burns
but that's my new thrill.
I'll practice with eyes closed
and mind open still.
Three months away
and I'll go all in at the show.
It'll be my death and I'll let my life overflow.)

The Show

The belly of the beast,
that's where true worship is done.
The waters are deep
and your legs weigh a ton.
A second chance to live,
another chance to fight.
When you can no longer write,
and only recite.
The first show,
the first blessing.
Just a microphone and a message.

Aura: "These poems are all
that the crooks never took!
This first song's called,
The Ground You Shook!"
An angry start,
like most young lives.
The large crowd was awe struck
as the folk lyrics cut like knives.
Their thoughts put into rhymes
and murderous metre.
They cheered for the young soul and believed in the believer.

Aura: "Now I'm going to slow it down,
just how life should be.
Working the nine to five
and praying to be free.
Dedicated to blues players,
songs of early morning aches.
The ones that talk about the Devil
and worse of heartbreak.
The crowd was surprised
at the slower pace.
It was a sound they missed and could never be replaced."

The last song was
the core of his anxiety,
A song of love and lust.
The cure and disease of society.
He took a deep breath
and thought of her.
How she was by his side
and knew every word.
He looked at her the whole way through
and she smiled on.
If poetry is the hill, she's the ground it was built upon.

Aura's set ended
and he was blessed with cheers.
Aura: (My mind's no longer blood soaked
with my very own fears.)
His gaze broke from Thothra
and there he saw the kudu, Kohen.
A calm figure
with all his colours glowing.
They mirrored one another
and moved in the same direction.
Meeting at the same point, to start a new lesson.

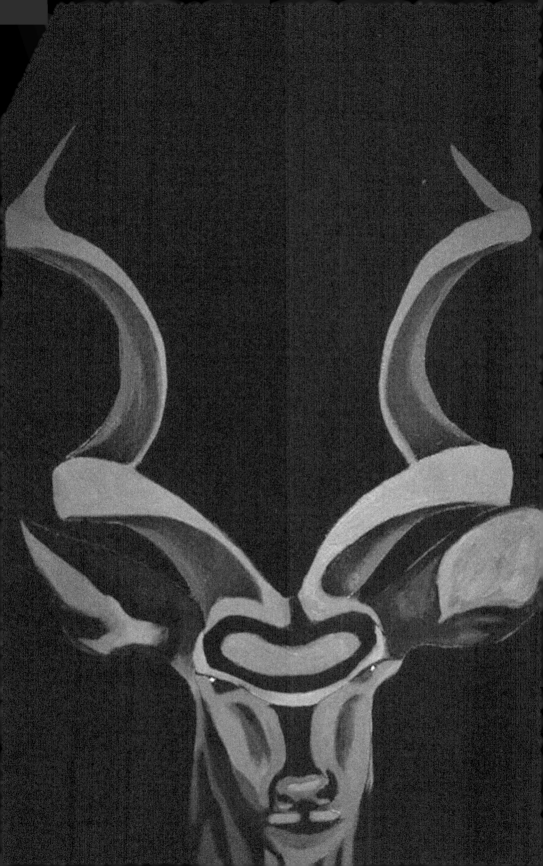

Guides

To live before death,
that is what we long to do.
To walk in the clouds
and soak in the view.
It could be a dark sky,
or one drowning in hues.
To be present with the wind
and not just passing through.
Many guides on this path,
we don't ever get to choose.
The best never give answers but lead us with clues.

Aura: "Mr. Kohen,
I've come a long way for you.
You see my mother is sick
and I need your truths.
I have lost all my colours
and I have lost my self.
My whole tribes been bought
and put on a shelf.
I wish to restore their dreams
and give them back their hope.
To help them to their feet and untie their ropes."

Kohen: "I see you're swimming in ideals,
and that will not do.
You cannot restore their hope
but show that they have the same power too.
The silent spells
and the almighty symbols.
Those are the oppressors
two loaded pistols.
Your art will not do a thing
and your songs will all drown.
It's the act of change that will be your crown."

Kohen: "I was never like you
        and I mean that as a compliment.
        You are the next step in evolution
        and share my earlier accomplishments.
        We are from the same tree
        but you're a new budding branch.
        You are closest to the sky
        and the Sun's lonely dance.
        There is nothing I can do for you
        and that is the truth.
        Your colours are returning because of your drive to improve."

Kohen: "I'll tell you the story
        of the one before me.
        Larger and wiser
        yet unknown with little glory.
        We called him Woody
        but I don't know if that was his real name.
        You see back then,
        no one wanted the fame.
        He picked up his instrument
        and lived on the road.
        No belongings and not a single dollar owed."

Kohen: "He lived with nothing,
        sang with nothing
        but gave the world
        his everything.
        His music quietly lingers,
        it has been changed to many forms.
        He could not save a soul,
        but he ignited a burn.
        You can't just be a frail
        ripple in this ocean.
        Be as the stars, still but in constant motion"

Kohen: "We will now write together,
with no motive attached.
You cannot lift the world's burdens,
you will only break your back.
You will naturally inspire the youth;
dreams can come true.
The downtrodden will realize
they can still run without shoes.
You have heard this before,
now please take a deep breath.
We will conquer life by forgetting of death."

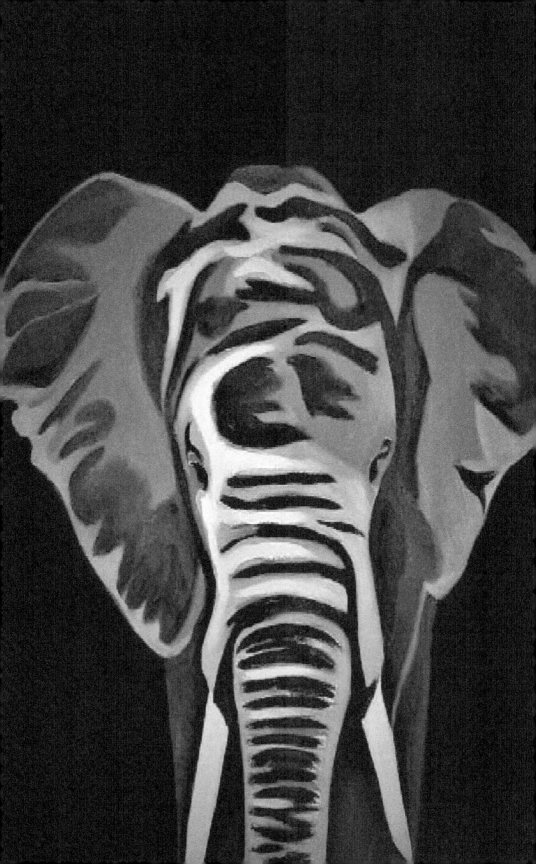

Redemption

A new colour palette
and an old brush will do.
The act of creation is personal,
and sacrifice is due.
Years of suffering,
days of joy.
Years of creation,
days of destroy.
A caterpillar is forgotten,
and the butterfly is praised.
A caterpillar is born, and a butterfly is obtained.

Kohen: "When you go back,
        you will have to fight.
        These beasts will not let up,
         they grow stronger with fright."
  Aura: "I left my people,
        for what?
        I cannot shake
        these razorblades in my gut."
Kohen: "Your solitude was necessary.
        it is what your people wanted.
        Chasing your dreams represented throwing down the gauntlet."

Kohen: "Go back with your love,
        your colours and music.
        Show the world their chains
        are but an illusion.
        I will go back with you
        and so will your new friends.
        We will be by your side
        until these beasts make amends.
        Woody will also come,
        see he's not just a legend.
        He's stronger now and knows the fruits of vengeance."

Homeless

Stepped on,
broken and still alive.
This is what torture
must be like.
Talent consumed
by greedy fools.
The house always wins,
that's why I don't play by their rules.
The way back home
is always short.
Even with a crack in the foundation, it will always support.

Aura: "All my new friends,
you were all my teachers.
You have molded my mind
and hardened its features.
Now you wish to travel back with me
and help my people.
I vow to pay you back
by maintaining this steeple.
We'll now march
for peace and not war.
We march for the future and long to breathe by its shore."

(Crowd cheers. Aura and Kohen perform)

Kohen: "The work of our hands sculpt
the past, present and future.
We will always be in control,
no matter the proclaimed ruler.
These are beasts
we all must defeat.
We will raise hell
and burn them with heat.
We are the center,
that has been forgotten.
All individuals and that is enough to have in common."

Cold Beginnings

Furthest thing from God,
a human.
Death never sleeps,
she's forever looming.
A light is always shining
yet it always seems dark.
It's somehow so icy
on this melting blue rock.
The beginning is cold,
and that is how it goes.
A bird is set free when it begins to snow.

Aura found himself ecstatic
on his travel back.
The entire flock's heartbeat pounded
and shook the dirt track.
Suddenly a quiet wind
could be heard in the valley.
The birds lost their voices
and whispered sadly.
The signs began to stand out,
Aura began to run with force.
A head on a stake and he denied the source.

His father dead,
no his father slain.
He prayed for anger
but his mind began to rain.
He had flashbacks
of the good days.
How his father did all his duties
and always looked unfazed.
Now his head before him,
still with that heroic gaze.
Completely lifeless, yet his courage remained.

Aura fell to his knees
and not a single noise.
Aura: (We've lost our harmony
and now the beasts will destroy.
I was so close
and the first sign of death…
The first sign
and I've already swallowed my breath.
What did this man do?
Who did he ever anger?
The good crucified… who designs these disasters?)

Kohen: "We ride for the good
and all that they have done.
Your father's story will be remembered,
the next chapter is his son.
I'll tell you the truth about your father,
he and I go back.
He was alone on the road
and I was on the same track.
We were both starving
and we inevitably locked horns,
He could've had me by the neck but he calmed his storm."

(Flashback)

Nova: "Your colours are different,
what purpose do you serve?
How could I kill something so unique,
I feel your individuality shall be preserved."
Kohen: "I was born this way,
I don't know anything about purpose.
I sing for my pride
and give hope when they're hopeless.
You are a wolf
and I am your prey.
Will this world not fall apart if you decide not to slay?"

Nova: "I'm a lone wolf,
       you see I only eat when I need to.
       I've buried societies peer pressure
       and carry my own view.
       I've also never fit in,
       let the truth be told.
       I feed this flame,
       it keeps me from being cold.
       If you sing, I want you to know.
       I don't care for your voice.
       I write poetry myself, it's the inscribed vows I enjoy."

Kohen "How far can we go,
Sings: with our dreams in our pockets?
        Dust in our ears
        and we can't hear the knocking.
        Not our guitars
        but our arms that we are strumming.
        Forced in the fire
        and burned from the rumblings.
        Trapped seeking truth
        in a pit full of liars.
        We lose our minds like a bird on the wire."

Nova: "That's it,
       that's music to my ears.
       Food for thought,
       that is what I adhere.
       Here's my scrapbook,
       I think it's better off read.
       You'll read about my fevers
       and the times I lost my head.
       I'll have to follow my ancestor's path
       and join a pack instead.
       Let my dreams travel with you, as to me they are dead."

Kohen: "These scraps of dreams,
        I'll carry with me.
        The world should know all perspectives
        and what they mean.
        I've done good my whole life
        and nothing good has come of it.
        It's time to rise
        and never submit.
        I'm sure I'll see you again
        and I will repay you.
        May it be a time of change, a time of new."

(Present)

Kohen: "Aura,
        I want you to have this book.
        Read the similarities,
        learn from the outlook.
        He was just like you,
        but born of a different time.
        Both born at the bottom
        and wished to climb.
        He became the preserver,
        a different kind of success.
        You must first destroy to get out of this mess."

Wicked Counsel

Building laws
and living above them.
The gravest weapons
cannot be seen.
Tricked and deceived,
this war cannot be won
with masks stitched to our faces
and muted tongues.
Rebelling leads to heroes
being treated like criminals.
Rebelling leads to crucifixions but also miracles.

Apopsis: "I hear their feet pounding
and I can't help but grin.
These fools don't know
we wear no moral skin.
Seth call forth the front line,
make sure it's the youngest.
Arm them heavy to the teeth,
let's leave their wills crushed.
They are all tired and thin,
they will do anything for food.
Threaten to take their jobs and spread fear through the news."

Jinn: "Rumor has it that
the young pup has grown.
He met Astar up north
and devoured him into bones.
The pup has wings
and he has begun to soar.
Oh how we've been so entertained
by the determination of the poor.
Let us send Preta to the front,
that vile and hungry ghost.
She's afflicted by hunger and loves a bloody roast."

Abraxus: "Let us also send the pup's sister,
　　　　　it'll make an entertaining plan.
　　　　　Decorate her with shiny armour,
　　　　　so he can't recognize her scent or hands.
　　　　　We'll send them both
　　　　　and that will be enough force.
　　　　　They have more numbers,
　　　　　but evil outweighs their source.
　　　　　War is for the ruthless ones,
　　　　　these artists won't stand a chance.
　　　　　Our tools have been sharpened; these fools only use their hands."

Front Lines

There is a dynasty behind
every introspective cigarette.
Drowning in the front lines,
it's easy to forget.
Empires are built
with blood and blueprints.
An uprising is nature,
It keeps the world in sync.
Bundled up for slaughter,
and muzzled by the cold.
All it takes is one brave voice for the whole world to be heard.

Aura, Kohen
and the ones from up north,
stood like shadows on the border
and resembled the slopes.
Then came armoured wolves,
ravens and other beasts.
All in perfect formation
and never skipping a beat.
Actor: "What a waste of time
and potential.
Could've dreamed with that discipline and lived in an adventure."

Aura: "We are bona fide beings!
Don't be fooled by this peacocking!
Planned confidence,
you can hear their knees knocking.
Anyone of them that is not beast
is one of my people.
Use your spells to subdue them,
strength can be peaceful.
I will go after their leader,
I will rip off that grey helmet.
Fight as resilient individuals, to evil that is overwhelming."

Aura and Dharma
met in the center of the war.
With demonic persistence
and the heroism of folklore.
Their strikes
had the authority of thunder,
yet with calmness
and experience of hunters.
They both laughed,
they both laughed in joy.

Aura: (I'm living my childhood, which adult wouldn't be overjoyed?)

Their fight went on
and all were at awe,
then Aura struck
with a vicious claw.

Aura: "Dharma!?
Is that you?
What's happened to your eyes!?
They are not like I knew."

Dharma: "Aura!
I could never forget that voice!
They blinded me with one of their rituals of choice."

Dharma: "They thought they could kill me
by enlisting me in the army.
I overcame my blindness
and vowed that no one could stop me.
I had to work with them,
what else can a caged animal do?
They sold us freedom
and brainwashed us in this zoo.
Told us your new friends are the enemies.
Your voice! Howl my brother!
They are ready to rebel and embrace new colours."

(Aura howls an old folk song)

All the animals threw down
their burdensome shells.
They all roared
and burned away their spells.
All that is left now,
are those abiding beasts.
Small in number,
but murderous elites.
The animals raised their chins
and stood proudly by Aura's side.
Aura: "We'll chew through these demons, with a demonic appetite!"

Ghosts

Flowers for romance,
flowers for death.
Paintbrushes to create,
paintbrushes to make mess.
A sharp thin line
between all things.
Look how harmless the bee is
without its sting.
If only this line
could be seen.
We wouldn't be harmed trying to understand what all this means.

Aura prowled forward
towards Preta's stronghold.
It was surrounded by beasts
and a dreadful mold.
His companions charged the beasts
with no anxiety in mind.
Aura hopped into Preta's wagon
leaving all his thoughts behind.
Aura: "I've heard of you hungry ghosts
and I've waited for this moment.
I'll conquer you as the hawk does the rodent."

(Aura fully extends his wings destroying Preta's wagon)

Preta: "I've watched over you
and I never sensed fear.
What made you so confident
that I would never appear?"
Aura: "This land is run amok
with folk tales and legends.
I've learned it's best to create your own
and treat the past as lessons.
Here you are before me,
tumbling like a tear drop.
I'll rip you to shreds, our fight for freedom will never stop."

(Aura slays Preta)

Aura: "This one tortured the minds of our children,
      but no more.
      If something is rotten,
      we must destroy its very core.
      Let us march to Abraxus
      and his enduring followers.
      We'll blind their eyes,
      what good are their watchtowers?
      For all the time they've stolen,
      we'll get back double.
      I swear our calloused hands will turn them into rubble."

Family

This world turns
even siblings to rivals.
A happy family
is a mere group of survivors.
The little conversations,
that are always missed.
Memories are frozen
and concealed in life's mist.
They divide and conquer.
Comradery is to fight the system.
Born with the same struggles, we just look a little different.

Aura: "Dharma, how is Mom?
Is she all right?"
Dharma: "She was down when Dad passed,
but lately she's been bright.
She does everything in his name,
including not giving up.
She doesn't wrestle with ideals
and that why she hasn't let up.
Everything happens for a reason…
No, things just happen.
She lives in this world now, recognizing life is worth having."

Dharma: "The music you made up north,
she heard it down here.
It eclipsed her depression
and cleared her tears.
She repeats daily,
Nova will live through his children.
We'll bury these demons
and expose all that is hidden.
I can't explain to you my anger,
I sometimes lose myself.
We were happy for mere years, I've forgotten how all that felt."

Aura: "Please sister,
      I could never survive your pain.
      You've been blinded by venom
      and wedded to a ball and chain.
      You are a titan
      and you will get through this.
      You are a giant amongst insects,
      with rain you will get hit.
      Let's fight back
      with peace and purpose.
      Let's win the world back by cleaning the rot off her surface."

Aura: "Please meet Thothra,
      she has our tribe's soul.
      Helped me understand life's fragments
      and taught me to be whole."
Dharma: "Isn't he such a hopeless thing?
      Always so serious.
      He always rejected bands,
      now he's no longer delirious."
Aura: "Thothra's with child now,
      it's hard not being solemn.
      We are driven with this fire to right this new Sodom."

Thothra: "It's a pleasure to meet you
      and your entire family.
      He's always so hopeless,
      I tease him happily.
      I've never seen such hopeful land,
      for our children we will win it back.
      These beastly pyramids
      are all meant to crack.
      Let us camp here tonight,
      we have much to celebrate.
      Let's sing songs and dance, our fire will resonate."

Abraxus

On top of every mountain,
it is smoldering cold.
Not all things are worth the price,
just ask the man who sold the world.
The supreme good of the Sun,
it all goes for naught.
Nights are longer than days,
the light must be lost.
No reflection in this mind's mirror
just demons throwing fits.
Some die fighting, others do not bother to resist.

Abraxus: (Not a living being
knows my true power.
I am no way near heavenly
but I rest in the highest tower.
This Aura will devour us
but only in flesh and skin.
They don't know that I am
the darkness that travels within.
They will be laying camp soon
and I will pay his love a visit.
I'll possess every inch of her and turn her into my peasant.)

Taking Over

Demons don't
discriminate.
Young or old,
I will germinate.
An orchestrated coup,
is always swift.
Very few ever turn down
the Devil's kiss.
Good versus evil,
life's greatest sport.
To reach for the stars and not fall short.

Abraxus made his way
to Thothra's tent.
She was massaging her belly
while lying in bed.
He appeared
with one claw over her mouth.
With a twinkle in his eye,
the other claw on her gut.
Abraxus: "I've known you since birth
and you don't know me.
I've watched from the inside, like the Earth watches her trees."

Abraxus: "You and your love,
you've gone too far.
I will have it my way,
I won't leave a scar.
When I enter you,
you will still be conscious.
I will control your body,
the torture for me is righteous.
Say a prayer, say a prayer,
I enjoy that noise.
It has not saved a soul, oh those meaningless ploys."

Like a rag doll he marched
Thothra to his citadel.
The Sun turned its head
and night grimly fell.
Her soul was crying
but he wouldn't allow a tear drop.
The world was his harvest
and she was a measly crop.
Abraxus:"The dead never get older,
I am as strong as ever.
All things rot, when I control the weather."

Gone

Where does this wind blow
and where does it all go?
I wonder if rain drops
ever wish they were snow.
Light to dark,
flesh to rot.
The games to cheat death
and not get caught.
Bodies on top of bodies,
spoiled are the crows.
When the light runs out, how will one grow?

Aura arrived late in his tent
to the smell of smoke and decay.
A ghastly perfume,
that only varmints could display.
He saw that Thothra was gone,
he already knew what had happened.
He closed his eyes
and did not panic.
Aura: (I've been here before,
life's just running its course.
I won't back down, I'll fight back with force.)

Aura: (Victories last but mere minutes,
my Father wrote this.
Demons don't play by rules,
that is their bliss.
The good get punished
but it's not a weakness.
It's an opportunity to overcome
misery and sickness.
My love is strong
and I trust she will not break.
She is different, she'll never abide to a snake.)

Aura: (I will rally the troops,
       I am but a mere symbol.
       They are the true source
       that cannot dwindle.)
       Aura meditated on the next leap,
       he wasn't sure that he slept.
       But as the Sun rose,
       he was sure what to do next.
       He woke his troops with a song.
       "The Eve of Destruction."
       For no wind, fire or rain would change their direction.

Hell's Mouth

All of yesterday,
I wanted tomorrow.
Now here I stand,
with an odd glow.
I plan on trading in
these thoughts for a tiny seed.
One that can be planted
and become all I need.
Today I stand loud,
and change it all.
For I know the way and don't fear the fall.

Aura stood tall at the gate,
with his wings upright.
It was the break of day
but cold like night.
He felt a calm madness,
very few will understand.
He was just inches away
from chopping the Devil's hands.

Aura: (I'll win everything back,
for they only left the crumbs.
They will witness the weakness, that comfort becomes.)

Aura
(Shouts):
"We will cure ourselves
of all lifeless fevers.
Let us break these chains!
For all the dead dreamers!"
They poured into the gates,
with smirks of fire.
They felt no fear of fiends,
like old church choirs.
He went for the head,
as his father taught him.

Aura: "Abraxus is mine, I'll bury him deeper than sin."

Struggle

The first and last breath,
are the same.
You'll leave as you came in
with no name.
A wandering fly in your mind,
a sleeping giant in your heart.
Wisdom to create
and wisdom to tear it apart.
The teachers live on,
only they are immortal.
They'll live through their students; infinite is the circle.

Kohen and Woody charged
at the younger demons below.
Woody   "These fiends went all in
(laughing): and now they live as unknowns.
Imagine trying so hard
and never having an abode.
We are the real rebels,
precious are our horns.
We angered both sides
and never pledged any devotion.
The animal is strongest with tamed emotions."

Apopsis: "Look at these old men,
frail skin and bones.
Have you ever thought,
some strive as unknowns?
Your time is up,
we will rewrite history.
You'll disappear from the books,
birthed in mystery.
We've erased many tombs
and torn down many statues.
Fragments of the past, your death is long overdue."

Kohen: "Your words hold no weight,
     crickets against the wind.
     These faces may crack
     but we'll forever wear these grins.
     I've fought the machines
     your ancestors crafted.
     Here I am,
     this rebellion's captain.
     Blind cats
     lost in a lion's den.
     It's up to us to show mercy or chew on your heads."

Apopsis charged
like a ram in its season.
Kohen lowered his horns
and charged like a demon.
They met with fire
and the smoke of thunder.
Apopsis lay lifeless,
his entire company felt a shudder.
Kohen's horns grew
and the others understood the logic.
He slayed many demons before creating anything melodic.

The Peak

A folk song
that never gets old.
The lonesome hero
lastly turns to gold.
Evil is here,
the jury is still out on good.
Still useful is the empty trunk
of the cottonwood.
The last breath,
before it is over.
The echoing applause after the shows closure.

Aura entered the darkest room,
lit by one dim candle.
He saw Thotra's shadow
and how it had been shattered.
Aura howled with rage
and the candle exploded.
The room shined of colour
as if darkness was broken.
Abraxus stood in front of him
as he always did.
They both smiled as they knew this was it.

Aura made the first move
and dove at him headfirst.
Abraxus was surprised
and uttered a curse.
Out came crowds of dead bodies
that Abraxus hid behind.
Abraxus: "These are all your ancestors,
this is the game I designed.
They were meek like you,
maybe you have put up a fight.
I've been here for years, what good is your bite?"

Aura: "Hide behind your shields,
        my instincts instruct me on what's real.
        They all died with honor,
        indulgence was never their meal.
        You never broke these kings,
        they never once caved.
        Keep their flesh 'n' bones,
        they've already been saved.
        This material world you rule,
        it stands no chance.
        We'll blind you with colour, our induced trance."

        Thothra shook off the curse,
        a soul defying slumber.
        A flame burned inside Aura
        and he remembered why he loved her.
Aura: "Abraxus,
        now I know you're weak!
        Here you sat in comfort,
        nowhere near the mountain's peak!
        Your curses are vanity,
        my wife now stands stronger.
        You've lost your support, just an aging warmonger."

Aura: "As the other beasts die,
        your darkness becomes clear.
        Remember I am a different wolf,
        I can smell a demon's fear."
        Abraxus laughed
        and spat out poison.
        The bile destroyed Aura's wings
        and left him boiling.
Abraxus: "You fool,
        I am the Sun's fire!
        Religion 'n' violence, I am the Devil your God hired!"

Thothra ran to Aura's side
and gave him a kiss.
Thothra: "Regardless of loss,
          you were built for this.
          I am with child
          but I will fight with you.
          We will live those rebel rhymes
          that we once drew.
          We'll fight on the same wavelength
          and relentless rhythm.
          A unified whole, a lethal composition."

Thothra charged left
and Aura charged right.
Aura let out a colourful glow
and focused his sight.
Abraxus had no choice
but to look his way.
His colour of red vanished
as he turned to grey.
Thothra clenched the back of his neck
and bit down with might.
Aura clenched the front of his neck with his eyes closed tight.

Abraxus,
A worm caught in a heat wave.
Laid brittle and broken,
meet Death's new slave.
Thothra felt a feeling in her stomach,
she couldn't describe.
She didn't want to take from the moment,
so she kept it inside.
They both opened their eyes
and softly stood tall.
They both locked lips and expressed it all.

Crown

A golden crown
on a greying mind.
Paradise is found
when you're running from time.
The chasing stops
and you finally look behind.
How far you've come,
how high you've climbed.
A sigh of relief,
Only you will ever hear.
Now it's just you and the music swimming in your ears.

Dharma was crowned
the new leader of Yellowknife.
With Luna by her side,
a faultless still life.
A dream when your past
is triumphed by your present.
Dharma now symbolizes
the strength of reinvention.
The whole village strived,
and no one fell behind.
War was forgotten and created was peace of mind.

Dharma: (My first goal
is to bridge the gap.
The North and South will meet
and complete the map.
This bridge
will not be exclusive.
Every being
will have their own music.
The chanting of the wind
and the cheers of the Sun,
will no longer be drowned as the war is now won.)

Endless

The crickets lose
their mystery in the Sun.
Life's lifelessness
cannot be out run.
A child is a new beginning,
a new glimmering hope.
That one can live
and untie the rope.
The powerless parents,
all they can do is watch.
As their offspring crawls to the very same clock.

The new pup was born
with jet black hair.
With an untiring appetite
and eyes so rare.
Only Aura's singing
calmed the boy.
The music filled in
a very dark void.
The young one was born
without a litter.
The entire town spoke of bad omens and a cold winter.

A new soul to wander,
a new soul to get lost.
A new soul of silence,
a new soul of thought.
The parents paid no mind
and did not worry.
They've learned moments like this
start a new a story.
Thothra and Aura decided
they would live on the road,
not homeless but as if all was their home.

Miscellaneous Poems

Designed

We're back together like rain in the water.
As we grew older this town grew smaller.
Now here we are, drowning with the rest.
Together but alone in this mess.

We've paced back and forth,
we've worn out our shoes.
We've bathed in many colours,
yet all that remains are the blues.

We're both shackled and muzzled.
Almost laughing at this struggle.
We almost made it out but sank in this sand.
A drop of water in this desert, who could withstand?

We've paced back and forth,
we've worn out our shoes.
We've bathed in many colours,
yet all that remains are the blues.

Like drunks, we have to call it quits.
Like drunks, we probably won't remember this.
You head your way and I'll head mine.
We won't blame each other, just the way we were designed.

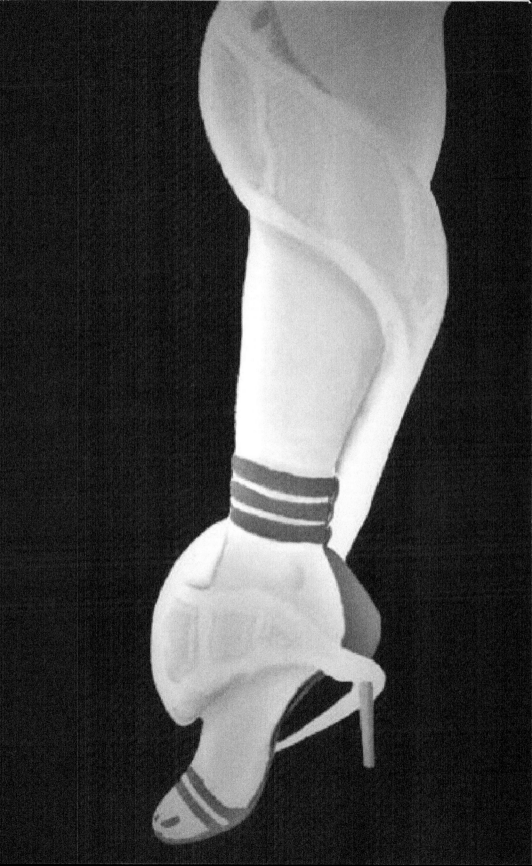

A Trade

Look, I noticed your dark sayings that I will need.
You see, I need to write about life and her duality.
All those swords are sharp and I'm thinking that is how the pen should be.
I've read the books and yes, sometimes even on my knees.

The new world may take it the wrong way and who am I to blame them.
Everything is so hyperbolic now, a writer can't beat this old drum.
I don't wish to take everything literally, my imagination keeps me numb.
I want to paint with both worlds and see the outcome.

Maybe if I wrote in fragments, I could represent the whole.
I'm not writing for my eyes, understanding is the reader's goal.
These are for my friends who read to harvest control.
You can have what's in this briefcase and no, it's not my soul.

Moonlight

I'm watching the Moon work and I can't believe what I see.
It flies like a sailor rebelling against his master's decree.
The clouds don't seem to bother like satiated bees.
Tonight they admire the sky's lonely debris.

Throw down your cool stairway and let me come close.
I know your loneliness as only a poet knows.
It's always dark and they say that's how it goes.
At least you're not suffering by wearing the Sun's clothes.

I'll live in your tiniest crater and keep you company.
We can stay up all night and whistle symphonies.
Not a wasteland but a tranquil land is where I wish to be.
You know all the world's dark secrets; will you share them with me?

When the Sun comes up, it's you I will miss the most.
Your complexion and light is different I suppose.
For my shivers return and all my dreams begin to slow.
Nothing else could induce these thoughts with such a light dose.

New Home

Death and all her friends behind this door.
Love, we now have a new home.
We'll cut the grass and wash the floors.
We'll be free and at times alone.
Let's free the poems from inside these drawers.
No furniture. we'll dance and roam.
Let's open the windows and allow in the Sun's scent.
Let's make most of our little descent.

All our neighbours will think we're functioning crazies.
Yet they won't know a thing or hear half of it.
For these walls are soundproof and their eyes cannot see.
How we've done things even the snake wouldn't permit.
We'll play in every room, our little sinning spree.
We've bit the apple, how could we ever quit.
We may get caught but they will still never know,
how it feels like to live behind these ancient doors.

Late at Night

John was up and out one night at an old friend's birthday.
Tom had invited his forgotten friends that used to learn and play.
Reunited in a crowded bar, Tom doubted John.
"How could you be so happy, when all you've done is write songs?"

John explained he worked like everyone else but also wrote for an hour day.
It wasn't about the money or to put on any kind of display.
John knew his arrogance; he could read it in his rhymes.
The group kept on drinking and in John's head he heard a chime.

The group asked John to sing and they began to mock him.
John again with his arrogance, "I don't sing on a whim."
Tom said, "Let's go out for a walk, that very park we used to run around in."
They all went out and that's were their true nature would begin.

"Hey believer boy, sing us a song. We just want to be entertained."
John felt he woke up, when he realized just how much they had all changed.
John sings, "Just like a tree planted by the water, I shall not be moved…"
A bottle flew smashing John and he lay bleeding out his wound.

John felt nothing and did not feel the need to defend.
He was bleeding by an old tree and thought he heard the voice of a departed friend
"Please don't worry, you were the closest and you will have it all."
Now John lay there dying and smiling, "Everything looks so small."

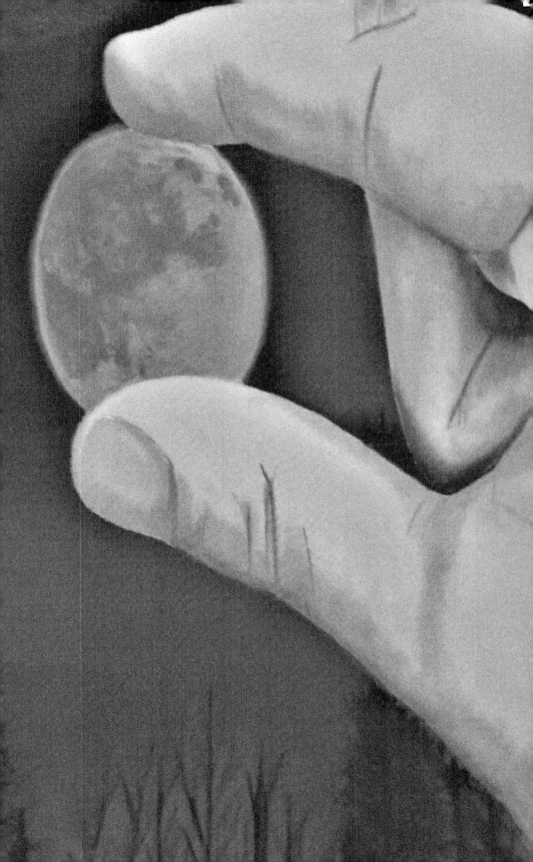

Inspiration

Where does it go?
I mean, it was just here.
I took only two bites of this magnetic meal.

All the thrills are gone
but I'll commit and finish it,
just one more hit.

Now that songs playing!
I'll repeat it over and over,
until the melody is sober.

It's beginning to pour out now.
Damn that noise is loud,
but it'll softened like a cloud.

Everything fades.
I wish it wasn't this way.
Maybe sometimes just not today.

In Wintertime

In wintertime up north
the wind injects me with fear.
For this was the time father left,
I dread having anyone near.
This snowman brings me cheer.

Here on Christmas morning,
always doubted Santa would appear.
I zipped this jacket up myself
as loneliness whispered in my ear.
This snowman brings me cheer.

My mother calls for me
and I smile as much as I can.
I built this snowman for her,
she told me Dad was a cold man.

This snowman brings me cheer.

Mantle

We worship these golden horns as if they've set us free.
They've poisoned us like the salt swimming in the Dead Sea.
Dead hours, raped clocks and rigged rules.
How could subsistence become so cruel?

Money around our necks, chains at our feet.
The moon's face has turned away; we've lost that treat.
Endless nights, sweating beasts and dying dreams.
Could we not rebel this bull's regime?

Moloch's head on a mantle, a quiet victory.
That captive bell has lost its burning witchery.
Bright days, alive times and loving lives.
Maybe this is where living begins?

No more dreaming in the dying dark.
All the fruits are hung in reach at this park.
Calm nights, conscious sleep and strong synergy.
Who would have thought of these liberties?

The Fight

I've grown tired fighting this bull who wishes to pierce my senses.
Claws of lusts, I was expecting the fight to end after adolescence.
I don't mind the other wounds; all scars tell a story.
I don't over indulge much but I'm force fed every politicians glory.
Pride and greed, I was told this would make me a man
but it's left me feeling like a school bus driver with no hands.
I'm crashing in all directions.
Now my rage is living in this collection.
Who do I take this anger out on? My family?
Selfishness; this system got me thinking of me, me, me.
I'll fight and I'll fight.
Then I will write, I will write.
To what end or purpose?
Maybe that other burning souls will help me out of this furnace.

Health

Spent years working on this body
in front of a lying mirror.
Now that it speaks things became clearer.
Mental health has no reflection.
A mind sharpens outside of the house.
Adventure is not a mistress but a loving spouse.
An exercise of selection.

Dream
(Writing at night)

The fallen tree became a bridge.
Crossed it with both eyes closed,
even if it was the size of a tight rope.

Blinded the darkness with a shard of light.
Spoke to the glowing sheep.
He said, "Wake up! Go live your dreams while they sleep."

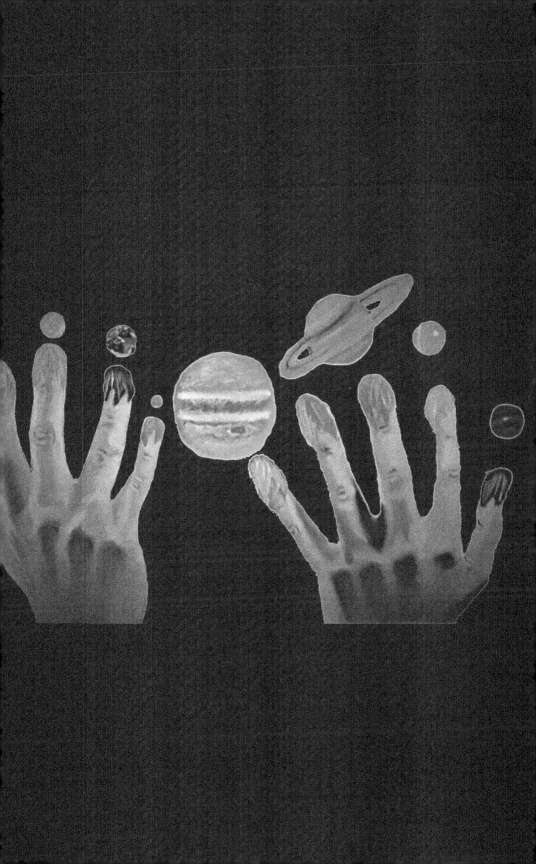

Dress Rehearsal

The mirror where I pretend to plan,
My already scripted play.
The razorblade butterflies flutter
and won't go away.
Trapped in the stomach
and work upwards to the mind.
All is blackened now,
as the eyes rusted and went blind.
The last glimmer of hope
is that this is all a joke.
A tragic comedy
concocted
When God woke up and spoke.

Freedom

Barbed wires slowly become enticing,
Twisted to harm.
Twisted to oppress.
With a calm hand can be less frightening.
The red residue.
The initiation.
It's the sacrifice that is enlightening.

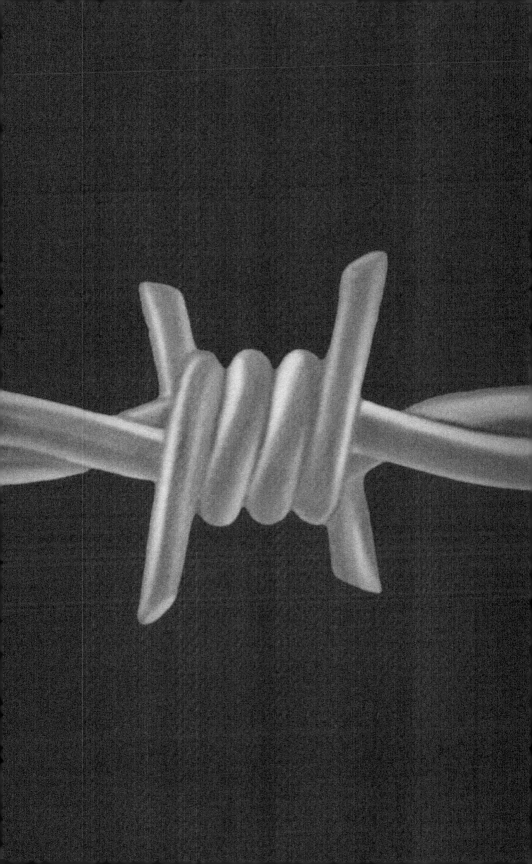

Seven Shells

The first is loaded, it is the time.
My mind is mangled. My only crime.
I could turn back now, the questions why?
My final vows. Son, please don't cry.

Loaded the second, forget the first.
We were born reckoned. Crucified 'n' cursed.
Born into our graves, where we decayed.
Our will departed. Our tragic play.

The third is cocked, I'll set us free.
We were always mocked. Living like fleas.
What could've been, is what they'll ask.
Photograph the scene. Bury the past.

I'm on the fourth, I had no choice.
Worked back 'n' forth. Neva' had a voice.
I loved them dearly, all I ever had.
Blinded by whiskey. Just a poor Dad.

Hurry to the fifth, can't take no more.
I'm feeling sick, I've lost the war.
The gods were watching, they always were.
Was always calling, but no one heard.

My love the sixth, promise no pain.
Never deserved this. My hopeful Jane.
You kept me alive, can't do the same.
Our love will survive, without the flame.

The seventh is me, a bludgeoned brain.
They'll analyze me, but not the pain.
Back into the wild, sentenced to go.
Just one last smile. Goodbye blue world.

Nursery Rhyme for the Racist

I want to meet the man.
I want to shake his hand.
I know he's not a fan,
that doesn't mean I can't.

He doesn't like my skin.
He'll always hate my grin.
May his next of kin,
see the colour within.

I wish to know his pain.
To wear it like a chain.
To show we are plain,
and also feel the rain.

He suffers the same abuse
and also fears the noose.
Prays to turn on the news
and not be the one accused.

One Time

The trees.
The flowers.
The silence.
The sky.
The birds
and the bees.
Everything seems so alive
in this cemetery.

Happy I come sometimes,
not just that one time.

Poet's Cafe

These eyes went blind,
hearing the poet's song.
Taught to enjoy funeral cake
as the gravedigger's violin shoveled on.
The prophets ran out of bread
and were drunk off wine.
As we continued to play
our rigged poker game of time.
The money stank of prostitute's perfume
and crows danced around dead doves.
The mask and tie are off.
The roots are poisoned by love.
Learned the world is made of paper.
The day my brother and I marked up the walls
and my mother smiled.
The roof in every room began to fall.
We never learned to pray.
I was lucky to knock on the right door.
Luckier to be let in.
The cafe where the poets write on the floor.
What is happening now,
that wasn't happening before?
Whistling tunes
and burying words.

She Could Never be Painted

Her and her warm hands,
remove the cover of sand
that I sleep under.
In pure still seconds
my frost was warm and I spoke,
it is a wonder.
Death comes when you're gone
and her arrows weigh a ton.
Only you can heal me.
Only you can feel me.
You are the ledge I hang from.
How strong and care free.

She could never be painted.
She is only seen through touch.
She could never be painted.
Only God knows her blush.

Her and her warm heart
beats the rhythm of all arts
that I struggle for.
In a swift moment,
inspiration floods my soul.
Leave me at this shore.
Seeing you in all,
I know of the bright antique light.
That put you before me.
That sat right beside me.
You are the stream I learn from.
How strong and care free.

She could never be painted.
She is only seen through touch.
She could never be painted.
Only God knows her blush.

Holy

What is holy?
Holy razor blade.
A very old razor blade.
One that was here before you.
One that is handed down, from scarred hand to another.
One that has long lost its sharpness but still serves the purpose it was made for.
One that will outlive you while you rot in a flower pot.
One that was here before you.
A very old razor blade.
Holy razor blade.
This is holy.

Dreamville

We are finally settled in this town.
We'll name the streets after those before us.
A colourful bird lifted our frowns
and placed in our hearts a pounding pulse.
We will pull our teeth and we will not ache.
We will discover all the truths we forgot.
We are here now but we won't call it fate.
Dead among us, lucky we didn't get caught.

Unclothed

My mind is snared by her skin.
Quiet secrets.
My eyes are strangled by her lips.
I've lost all my senses.
Am I crazy, for enjoying this?

Let's hear each other with our eyes closed.
Place your hand here and see clear.
Feel what your heat composed.
We'll roll in love's light.
The universe unclothed.

Table Manners

We're both stranded,
with voices in our heads.
Let us be free,
by putting them to bed.
We won't need to wait
until we can start eating.
Nothing to pass around,
and we won't mind the seating.
Our bodies will sing
a mouth-watering tune.
Tonight we eat with our hands,
and forget the tablespoon.

Her Hills

The Sun brings out her colours
and shows me the way.
My lips utter devotions
as we begin to play.

These quiet hills,
I never wish to leave.
Bounded to this earth,
our daily reprieve.

That fresh aroma,
never lost in the breeze.
The music of love plays
as these hills are appeased.

These ancient hills,
the only magic we will know.
Admired in all seasons,
wind, rain and snow.

The Sun is sinking
yet you stay forever strong.
It is your endless horizon
that writes these songs.

Goodnight

You brought me in,
when I was out soaking wet.
Asked me to put out my cigarette
and handed me a coffee instead.

The world is asleep now,
let us live new and be.
Come closer with your eyes closed
and please don't say a peep.

Don't take this the wrong way
your clothes will look better at your feet.
We'll keep each other warm
and only wear these bed sheets.

Making Love

I feel like doing everything,
then lying around doing nothing.

Cuckold

Seven black birds in the sky,
the scorching Sun veils all the shade.
Don is always out working,
lost the will for love's dancing game.
His domesticated loves
been hiding in silver waters.
Losing her will to submissively float.
She's eying the builder with hands of a potter.

She's gone. She's gone.
She's back out on the sea.
She smiles, yes, she smiles.
In the arms of a sailor.

With blood he'll build a new arc,
this sharp and hungrier man.
The fangs of her eyes sank in
and inspired his hands.
The smell of dark wine,
new love and their echoing tone.
A golden arc for this rising flood.
A new sea to roam; a palace away from home.

She's gone. She's gone.
She's back out on the sea.
She smiles, yes, she smiles.
In the arms of a sailor.

Her New Job

It's a crime that you must wear that mask.
Confused and worn, already torn by the past.
Loved the music of the spheres.
Now chained to your desk pondering dead years.

You skimmed all that they told you to read
and never got a grasp of what you wanted to be.
Tricked to believe you had a chance in this grey world,
dulled your true colours and left you transformed.

Wearing that hidden cross that can be seen in your eyes.
Now another angel wearing the devil's disguise.
Hope that mirror never takes your glow,
and you free yourself from this show.

You

I felt like
a kicked puppy,
before I met you.

Sat beside me
and the city shrank.
All I needed was you.

I slept during prayers
and of course,
dreamt of you.

The very little
I understand of life,
I owe to you.

The Fibonacci flowers
and their perfume
remind me of you.

Here now
to catch the rocks
they spit at you.

From this day forward,
I vow that my last word
will be you.

Warm Affair

She flowed towards me too gracefully,
that's when I became bewildered.
She whispered the wind's secrets in my ears
and watered my perverted ailments.
Convinced me I was saved
and converted me for a sweetened moment.
My winter heart was finally warm
but longed to be frozen.
That's when I finally understood,
The chill is what keeps me from burning.

Extra

They dance and don't notice the flowers,
and they don't even hear the birds.
They only see each other's eyes,
they only notice each other's words.

On this park bench I fade,
In the background it gets blurry.
It's painful being the extra
in someone's love story.

They sing and don't notice the weather,
they even get the lyrics wrong.
They've sat and done nothing
but this is where they belong.

On this park bench I fade,
In the background it gets blurry.
It's painful being the extra
in someone's love story.

They forgot to get a bite to eat
but they will never starve.
They don't bother to ask questions,
for them life is solved.

Breakup

We're dead.
I'm done.
She said.

I cracked.
I cried.
He heard.

You can't.
You couldn't.
She said.

I'm gone.
Goodbye.
He heard.

Blue

Blue, I can't believe you were once my favorite colour.
You no longer compliment, you blacken it.
It was Red that was supposed to haunt me, not you.
It was Yellow that was to make me feel ill, not you.
Blue, you got darker. I liked you better when you matched the sky.
Grey is your hue, Blue. You've become more polluted than the river.

Whirlwind

Recall, clouds give both shade and rain.
What is done we'll have to appreciate.
The fire's not in us to burn our brain,
but under us to help us levitate.
The sharpened rocks are not seen from heaven.
Feet no longer blister when you have wings.
The Kings will be slain by plain peasants,
and the mountains we climb will turn into springs.
So please get up with your chin raised high.
Yes, you drowned in your thoughts
but that was life in disguise.

The Cliff

Loosely gripped,
but so hard to let go.
The left hand dangles.
The right hand's mangled
but refuses to let go.
The cliff is your friend.
Your foe's the vulture
that pecks at your hand.

Rain

You can always tell that it has rained.
You can never tell for how long.
All the balconies are drenched.
Close your eyes and rest on one.

Fireplace

Embracing exhales while everyone wonders,
how have we forgotten to honor these winters?
The winter waves are not overwhelming here
but brightly reminding of our balancing nature.

Family fingerprints warm by the fireplace's symphony.
The wool sweaters snooze silently on our infancy.
Our quiet culture accommodates all,
Slowly assimilating even during the snowfall.

Anxiety

Sometimes,
even the stars hide.
You don't think silence
gets nervous
before it speaks?
Thoughts shudder
at the idea of being seen.
Get used to it
that you will never be used to it.

|Mind|

Who is in my mind?
Have I met you before?
You sounded a little different
but I've heard this thought before.

Why do you live in my mind?
I thought you wanted to go.
Made me think to put 45 to my head,
where did that person go?

Why do you hide?
You have proven you can overwhelm me.
I'm guessing you'll be back home in a couple years.
Back to scream at me.

Thinking

I feel like vomiting,
every time I talk.
It's not something I ate,
but pressure from the flock.

I enjoy the silence
they call awkward.
It's not my fault,
it's just my voice is slaughtered.

Slaughtered by political correctness,
I now think what I cannot say.
How different would life be,
if life were the other way.

Natasha's Story

Natasha was her name, fitting in was her curse
and she feared being alone and old.
Doomed to rush into love as most lonely ones are
that is why this folk story is told.
All her friends had found love, but she wandered all night.
Online hoping it would come her way.
She thought she found the one, a man with everything
that could help her live her dreams all day.

She would ask him to meet but he never did oblige,
he would keep her close with his warm texts.
Then on one quiet night, he asked to chat on cam.
Of course she wanted to see what's next.
He kept on with his words, she was under his spell
and she could never ever say no.
He wished for her to show just a little bit of skin,
she liked him and wanted him to know.

Next day he was distant and she didn't know why,
she had done everything that he asked.
She then got a message that would change her whole life,
a threat to show the world all her past.
She gave in with soft tears and begged him to leave her.
The warmth vanished from his words like coal.
He then asked her to come to his new apartment
and she better not dare tell a soul.

She arrived at his place and she was blown away,
how could a creep be livin' like a king.
A dame answered the door and she looked just like her,
but she was detached and paper thin.
There he sat at his throne with a perverted smile,
"Hun I have a proposal for you.
Why don't you work for me and live like a quiet queen?
In my trade, I know all the who's who."

She ran for the far door but was struck by a thought,
he had her whole soul in his laptop.
She fell hard on her knees. Sickness in her stomach,
she felt as if her spirit had just dropped.
The things that happen next, I do not want to say.
Just say that no one deserves this fate.
A fiend will always be, this cold persuasive way.
Pray for the angels lookin' for a mate.

Conveyor Belt

There was a young hungry man, who desired for food and work.
He had no place to rest and his heavy head longed for a bed.
He wandered into a mosque, and met an Imam with a smirk.
"Welcome my young brother, how may I help you in God's homestead?"

"I have bounced from job to job, and I'm fed up with my life.
Could you please please teach me, what all of this really even means?"
"The one and only meaning, bury your questions and strife.
I can show you the way, you can work for me throughout your teens."

Aldaris lived in this mosque and read all he was told to.
Not a single question, he gave all of his heart to the cause.
"God's son you have really grown, a soldier you've nurtured into.
Let's teach you of our plan. They've mocked us with cartoons and their laws."

"There is a grand church up north that the people love dearly.
That's where we make a stand, with knives we will make them all repent.
One God has brought you to me, to teach them to see clearly.
Now let's get our revenge, we will not be the ones to lament."

Aldaris puked at his feet, backed away from the devil.
"You sick and vile man, who do you worship and labour for?
I will starve on these dark streets and not eat of your venom.
God's feeble impostor, it is shells like you that fuel the war!"

Three long cold nights all alone, fighting his God who watched.
"I must tell the police, or would that just anger this being?"
On his way to the station, saw the news that charred his heart.
Three innocent lives dead. Conveyor belt of blind believing.

Father's Warning

I'll teach you of dark-eyed ladies.
The ones who own these streets
They dance around you and they have
crushed the flowers at your feet.
They are not at all like mother.
Don't you ever fall for that trap.
The lesson before the lover.
Don't you fly towards that lamp.

I have seen innocent souls burn,
no one can forget that smell.
Rotting door of this dominion,
many before you have fell.
Stay far from that dark-eyed woman.
She's a gypsy wearing red,
more dangerous than a bullet.
She will tear open your head.

Drunk Cheer

Worked like a slave for this right here.
All these golden beers drown my ears.
Singings not for all they say,
I do this for me no pay.

Singers locked away, scream and shout.
Destroy those chains and toss them out.
Every word will set you free.
Every song has its own key.

I do not think she hears my voice.
It's the smile that gives her joy.
She's closer now and eager,
to let loose of her fever.

Singers locked away, scream and shout.
Destroy those chains and toss them out.
Every word will set you free.
Every song has its own key.

We're leaving now and still going.
On these dark streets we're floating.
We'll stumble to our bare beds
and won't think about what's next.

Soldiers

Dead bodies marinating the ground.
Cries of mothers muting every sound.
Parades for the soldiers, who deserve so much more.
May they return and not be ignored.

They'll be many speeches after this war.
But no, yesterday will never be restored.
Prayers for the soldiers, who deserve so much more.
May they return and not be ignored.

A fountain of dead dreams
races due to these regimes.
Medals for the soldiers, who deserve so much more.
May they return and not be ignored.

An ash tray full of aspirations.
A tower with no foundation.
Poems for the soldiers, who deserve so much more.
May they return and not be ignored.

Job Rides the Bus
(Job attempting to read a book while on public transit)

Today I learned that someone couldn't believe it was a Monday.
It was the bus ride home and I was surprised it took him that long.

I also learned that a 12-year-old broke up with his girlfriend.
This conversation was extremely urgent and needed the utmost enthusiasm.

I then learned that a character didn't make it. It was shocking because he was a
main character and the show invested a lot of time in developing his personality.

I then learned that the stock market hit record highs. If an individual invested
$10,000 ten years ago, he would still be poor.

I then learned it's best to just listen to music and write on the bus.

Letter

To the person who stole my backpack,

I hope you weren't too disappointed finding books that are better off
unread. I hope that the scraps of poetry are at least recycled.
I'm certain you "ouu'd" and "ahhh'd" at some of the drawings.
The lion cub eating his sick father was my favorite.

Sincerely,
Starving Poet in the food court

Diagnosed

Her body, Holy
Her thighs, Sacred
Her eyes, Visions
Her thoughts, Prophecy

Doctor: You've been diagnosed with innocence; your poor soul may never survive.
Mary: How long do I have?
Doctor: I will give you one year before they notice your symptoms.
Mary: They?
Doctors: Those that carry pornographic plier.
Mary: What could they possibly do to me?
Doctors: They'll try to do all that they've seen but sadly come up short.
Mary: So I'll live?
Doctor: Of course you'll live but you'll never be able to get away from them.

Shift

Day one begins like any other.
Tired and a bit strange.
The world is disguised as ordered
but everything's deranged.

One breath, two breaths
and now it's back to the pack.
Time to hide my true colours
and be the one in black.

The leader shows face
and give us all our orders.
We'll be divided
and sent to different corners.

Day two begins like any other.
Tired and a bit strange.
The world is disguised as ordered
but everything's deranged.

Break

Busy blur of the work week
brought you to this table.
The bench seems colder
but the scent of grass warmer.
You can finally hear yourself think
and your anxiety sleeps in peace.
The machine is quiet now
but programmed to repeat.
Evenings like this vanish
and mornings jump up.
Now back to the desert
where the poor are ate up.

Train Station

This train station smells of piss,
I'm sure trains don't smell like piss.
So, it must be all of us in this.

The smell of rot,
on those that have been bought
and shackled into a flock.

The homeless dancing.
The junkies laughing.
The middle-class acting.

Vacation

There is probably nothing more sinful than this hotel
but damn am I happy.

This food looks half cooked and taste like salt
but damn am I happy.

I cut my self shaving and have a sun burn
but damn am I happy.

I don't know who won last night's games
but damn am I happy

I left work with a full inbox
but damn am I happy.

Haven't snapped one picture yet
but damn am I happy.

Haven't wrote a single word down
but damn am I happy.

Machines

It's not about breaking free anymore,
it's simply about
not breaking.
To be stepped on,
crushed and then placed on a shelf.

There must be a way
out of this mess.
Still in one piece
and you'll be sold,
"that's a victory!"

The conveyor belts
will continue to churn
obsolete machines.
The workers aren't to blame,
but the men programming the machines.

Sorry,
not programming.
The men owning the machines
and paying pennies
for them to be programmed.

Markets

(Flesh for sale! ... Get your flesh for sale!)
Comes with a suit and laughs at all your jokes!

(Flesh for sale! ... Get your flesh for sale!)
Will do twice the work for half the pay!

(Flesh for sale! ... Get your flesh for sale!)
Fills your diversity quota and makes for great photos!

(Flesh for sale! ... Get your flesh for sale!)
Dresses to impress with a strong handshake!

(Flesh for sale! ... Get your flesh for sale!)
Will keep your old wandering eyes occupied!

(Flesh for sale! ... Get your flesh for sale!)

Sailing

The suspense has been lost,
we're taught the end first.
Our life is the cost,
and knowing is the curse.

A sailor must sail
but it's not determined at birth.
To try is to fail,
and comfort is the curse.

The masked ones sell us masks,
our souls quench their thirst.
To be like the past,
Our futures are cursed.

Concrete Jungle

The blue lions nibble on plastic flowers,
and the shiny pigs feast on their flesh.
Nature is lost here.
No ears to hear.
The bodies disappear before they fall.

The well-dressed are the worst behaved.
The beautiful are barbaric.
Nature is lost here.
No ears to hear.
The beasts have burned the books.

The innocent children eat grenades
and the birds are all grey.
Nature is lost here.
No ears to hear.
It rains hard on our sky high graves.

Tongue and Mask

Tongue and Mask,
the new Sword and Shield.
It's all a cartoon,
and reality is concealed.
Yes men with power,
obedience can be bought.
Killing with tongues now
and not needing the buckshot.
Words become manure,
fertilizing our minds.
Leaving worms in our heads,
feasting on headlines.
Hammers gnawing,
at our children's knees.
Born broken, bruised
and squeezed by greed.
The masks have made it clear,
the poor will always be poor.
The rich won't always be rich
and maybe that will settle the score.

Gnashing

Those that kneel at your feet
won't always keep you from
shooting yourself in the foot.
The ground you shook,
collapsed the roofs
of our nurseries.
The fear you instilled
kept the minds in
the fetal position.
The glass ceilings
will oppress the youth.
The glass walls
will suffocate us all.
I'm happy you got to build
your own casket.
May you rest naked,
while we starve at our dinner table.

Bullets

The victims different;
White, Black, Brown.
The settings vast;
School, Church, House.
The weapons countless;
Semi, Hand, Assault.
The motives many;
Money, Power, Revenge.
The news divided;
Hate, Illness, Religion.
The solutions vary;
Law, Gun, Restriction.
The heroes many;
Police, Firefighter, Paramedic.
The bullets similar:
Red, Red, Red.

Revenge

Lost on this mountain.
My mount crawls forward.
I'm wearing my father's armour
and it still doesn't fit.
This violent blizzard has
erased all my footprints.

I'm ready to face the thunder.
I'm ready to drown in rain.
This summits so far up,
but I still cannot see.
My frozen nature
is burning in the breeze.

This useless burden.
This permanent stain.
This everlasting wound.
I've hoped and prayed for scars.
I am pledged to this mountain,
like swine to a farm.

Tales from faraway lands,
many winters ago.
This way to my mind.
This way to the circle.
I know where I'm going,
doomed for another hurdle.

Compromise

I'm certain Mother Nature is kind,
that's why she chooses to compromise.
The woodpeckers peck on concrete
to give way to our fog of car horns.
The flowers melt swiftly
to allow our flower shops to remain full.
The trees are cut in half,
to make way for our forever incomplete highway.
Thank you.

Perfection

The symmetrical trees sicken Mother Nature,
she vomits at the sight of precision.
Amputated branches
to fit our standards of fulfillment.

The beauty that brought us here
and made us free to be.
The chaos that we've feared,
but is the source of our peace.

The dirt road stretches further,
far passed the perfect pavement.
It ventures past depression
and leads to our salvation.

The birds suffer due to our dependence,
nibbling on our excrements.
They slowly convert to rats
that forget their earthly testament.

The bulimic birds
aren't the only ones suffering from illness.
The chaos has been corrupted
and perfection is our sickness.

Books and Knives

The books on the top shelf
they whisper in our ears.
Visions that can't be seen
but will clear all our fears.
A sharp mind is not a weapon,
but a defense.
It allows us to see the shadow
beyond our visual sense.
The shadow that is a teacher
and a friend.
The one who will travel with us
until the very end.
Thank you books on the top shelf,
it's you that helps us pieces of mud
sculpt ourselves.

The Fly

The fly in my mind
knows me well.
Buzzing around my head,
I wonder what it smells?
Well, my mind's in the gutter
and it must smell the waste.
Anxiety's drying dung,
it must want a taste.
Disgusting creature
but who am I to critic.
The pieces I leave behind
is what it eats.

Getting over Writer's Block

(This one doesn't count)

That child smoking a cigarette isn't dumb, he's smart. He gets it.
I've decided to roll down the hill and not climb up it,
I'll meet you all at the bottom.
I wrote this for you,
I wish to place it on top of all the textbooks you don't read.
Blank canvases with oil paint splattered intestines.
Black pages with cocaine scribblings engraved as thoughts.
Muddy clay carved with machine guns and machetes.
4/4 bars crucified by car horns and screams of children.
Books screaming in pain as the libraries are raped.
The bought billionaires are all worthless.
Don't push the red button, smash it and rip it apart.
Lets go, Lets go, Lets go... My lord, my lord, my lord.
The roads are blocked but I will not stop.
The radio has one eye that keeps us locked.
The sun stings like a bee but the moon is just a creep.
Eye contact is where you build trust said the perverted salesmen.
The stranger is death. Do you huddle now because of love or fear?
"Son, were going to church"....."Now? It's midnight."
Lonely and bored, I actually went through my junk mail.
Assassination? No I'm not important. This is just plain murder.

Printed in Great Britain
by Amazon